THE
SECRETS
OF
PRECIOUS STONES

Ursula Klinger Raatz

THE
SECRETS
OF
PRECIOUS STONES

A Guide to the Activation
of the Seven Human Energy Centers
Using Gemstones, Crystals and Minerals

LOTUS LIGHT
SHANGRI-LA

The Author
Ursula Klinger-Raatz was born in 1950 and is a graduate teacher and
psychologist. Since 1970 she has been exploring the conscious use of
mental powers for self-healing and the expansion of consciousness.
Her progress has been marked by contact with spiritual healers of
many traditions, the teachings of India and those of the American
Indian peoples, as well as contemporary energy concepts. She has
been working independently with individuals and groups since 1983,
devoting herself to the unfoldment and realization of healing energies
using primarily gemstones and crystals.

1. American Edition 1988
by Lotus Light Publications
P. O. Box 2, Wilmot, WI 53192 U.S.A.

The Shangri-La series is published in
cooperation with Schneelöwe Verlagsberatung,
Federal Republic of Germany

Originally published 1986,
© by Schneelöwe Verlagsberatung, Durach-Bechen,
Federal Republic of Germany
All rights reserved
Cover design and illustration: Wolfgang Jünemann
Translation: Peter Hübner Verlagsservice
Editorial Supervision: Monika Jünemann
Production: Schneelöwe, Durach-Bechen, Fed. Rep. of Germany
ISBN 0-941524-38-8

Printed 1988 in the Federal Republic of Germany

This book is dedicated to the earth and all of its beings,
the powers and helpers of the spiritual world,
and Gila and Horst Krohne's oasis of light on Tenerife,
where the energies for the writing
of this book converged.

Table of Contents

Foreword

Precious stones, crystals and minerals still have their »secrets«, but it is by no means a secret anymore, that healing processes can be initiated by concentrating energy of consciousness. And with increasing frequency we meet people who have themselves learned to consciously employ the possibilities inherent in this for the purpose of healing and cognition, or are teaching this to others.

So the secret of precious stones merely lies in the way in which we know how to utilize them.

Everything is vibration; planets, people, plants and stones vibrate, too. The idea behind this book came from the realization that there are certain stones and certain energy centers in the human being, whose vibrations oscillate similarly and react to each other. This means that due to the oscillation frequencies of the colors of the stones, they influence energy centers having the same color frequencies.

Utilizing the concentrated energy of consciousness, we can therefore imbue the stones with the »symbolic content« that lets them become effective helpers and healers for us. By this process we increase our life energy, which has positive effects on all areas of our life, including the state of our health. Since each one of our cells is »consciousness«, we can influence each of them with our consciousness.

This provides us with unimagined possibilities for self-healing and for helping others to employ these methods. However, at this point it should again be stressed that all of the recommendations for »healing« certain ills made in this book are not meant to be understood as substitutes for medical treatment. It will not help, for instance, to try to treat diabetes by placing a certain stone on the corresponding energy center and waiting for something to happen. The purpose of the entire process would be totally misunderstood, and besides that, a person's health could be endangered if appropriate medication were not sought. Responsible use of precious stones is therefore in no case meant to replace medical advice or assistance.

The stones work in a different way: through our concentrated energy of consciousness. By using the stones we occupy ourselves more intensively with our illness or our emotional entanglements, through them our body is stimulated to activate its own capability for healing itself. Wherever the book refers to specific physical reactions, this is based on singular or multiple experiences and the intuitive use of a certain stone, an experience that may repeat itself and probably will, but does not necessarily have to.

In using the stones you will probably notice additional relationships of their effects on certain physical functions. You will learn from the stones, and recognize what you knew all along.

M. C.

Introduction

Through gemstones and crystals a door opened itself for me that led to new dimensions and realizations about correlations in the cosmos and their parallels in human nature. It is a great joy for me to be permitted to present this comprehensive store of knowledge, so that the subtle powers gemstones possess may be used meaningfully.

I was introduced to gemstones by a shaman who had received his initiation by North American Indians. The world of stones immediately responded to this and began to disclose itself to me. Since that time I learn most about stones by working with them. They teach me how to clean and to charge them, whom and how which stone can help, what it heals, which qualities it enhances, what it stimulates, how it should be worn and stored. Right from the beginning it was easy for me to comprehend this language, as I was already a channel for the universal force of life — divine love — and for messages from the spiritual world, as well as for sensitive perceptions of internal processes and structures, and was therefore familiar with the subtle energies. The stones joined in all of this as powerful helpers. They are prepared to support our efforts to achieve healing, spiritual growth and a greater measure of perfection.

Healing always occurs on several levels. This I can confirm through my own realization and experience with myself and my work with others, whom I was able to help. Sickness and disharmony of the body, as in thoughts and emotions, mirror difficulties on a mental and spiritual plane. It is therefore not enough to heal an illness on the physical level alone. Instead, each illness bears in it an indication of problems within our perception and our mental habits, because they determine our behavior.

Therefore an illness provides us with a chance to transform segments of our attitudes and behavioral patterns, to learn to act more meaningfully and in accordance with our life.

The body is the »densest plane« of our being that teaches us through pain what we do not yet perceive on the more subtle levels.

It is therefore my wish to help others to again become so watchful and sensitive that they will learn to recognize and heed the more subtle processes in themselves and become able to activate subtle energies.

When we avail ourselves of spiritual powers in our everyday efforts, the burden on our bodies will be eased, our minds will become calmer and more serene, our thought patterns experience positive changes, and creative abilities can unfold. We become more sensitive, our hearing more acute, our attitude towards ourselves and our environment more loving. We regain access to the sources of strength inherent in our souls, and can enter into conscious contact with our higher guide in the spiritual world. Our growing confidence in »being guided by divine wisdom« and listening to our inner voices becoming more natural, make it possible for us to »grow beyond ourselves«, to learn to activate and make use of energies for self-healing, self-development, self-realization and expansion of consciousness.

The stones help in their own way by letting our world become more transparent and comprehensible for us.

The messages that I am passing on in this book are not meant to be understood as prescriptions for the healing of certain illnesses or formulas for the development of certain capabilities, but rather as a guide for entry into the world of stones, which holds a lot more in store to reveal about us if we really immerse ourselves in it.

So this book should be considered an impulse for a way that via the stones will again put us in conscious contact with the wisdom and energies of life. And for this help and instructions are provided: For the use of gemstones and crystals for the benefit and creative development of Mankind, Nature and all of Creation.

Chapter I

The World of Gemstones and Crystals

When we examine the exterior of gemstones, we find an abundance of colors, shapes and patterns that nature has brought forth, uniquely concentrated and differentiated. Unlike human beings, animals and plants, they do not suffer sickness nor do they age in our sense of the word, they require no care, no water or nourishment to maintain them. They came into being through the Earth's mighty, primeval shaping forces, the fire it contains and the light of the Sun, water and the vibrations of the Moon, the air and the spiritual beings of the creative powers. In their development they experienced tremendous heat, pressure and solidification, but also demonstrated perseverance and patience while growing and collecting and condensing light. The most radiant and brightest of them additionally underwent a multitude of precise polishing processes at the hands of human beings. All of this vibrates in a stone, and the elemental forces that caused it to be as well as the form-giving processing that refined its shape, contain much to be learned for our own lives.

Each kind of stone was imprinted with an individual vibration during its creation, which is clearly expressed

17

by the color, but also the shape into which the stone grew or was brought by the hand of Man. This vibration is ceaselessly given off by the stone into the atmosphere. It is a very powerful, dense vibration, yet effective on the subtle, spiritual plane and therefore also reaching our consciousness as highly developed spiritual beings. We humans are the creatures on earth that increasingly learn to know and consciously apply their spiritual forms and capabilities, and are ever more attracted by the inner powers of the stones.

The effects of stones on human beings were already known in ancient cultures and religions, where they were used for healing and to invoke, hold and transmit certain powers. This potential remains the same, but in our time it needs to be applied in a new way, recognized more consciously, developed further and realized fully.

The stones bear in themselves the crystalized spirit of the Earth, to which we can gain access through our dedication and interest, each of us in his or her individual way according to our own needs and way of healing. Every stone − even those of the same kind − has an individual shape and pattern, and therewith unique vibrations and radiance capable of effecting each one of us differently. Not everyone needs a great and mightily vibrating stone in order to achieve great things. Occasionally a stone is in order that gives off very subtle yet purposefully directed vibrations. The same problem or matter of concern may in the case of one person be solved with a totally different stone or one varying in shape from that effective for another person, because each of us has his or her individual structure.

But to determine this a very differentiated individual and intuitive approach is already required in order to work with the powers of a stone, which do not avail themselves to everyone in the same degree right from the start. But the stones will teach us a great deal, once we have given them our attention and love and have made them a part of our lives. A basic vibration is emitted by their colors. Their appearance is naturally familiar to us, so that we can use them without further foreknowledge to enter into the world of gemstones.

That colors possess certain powers that effect us is a fact which we know not only from healing with stones, but from the teachings of color analysis and color therapy. In the stones we are faced with pure, natural colors. They were created in accord with nature and therefore transmit their perfect unity and harmony into us. So through gemstones we are put in touch with very clear, balanced vibrations that are capable also of re-establishing this harmony within our own physical, spiritual and mental vibrations.

Every color has its own frequency and even within these limits there are significant gradations between darker and lighter shades of a given color. All matter becomes visible through color, and the natural sciences have long ago proven that matter consists of vibration constantly oscillating. How we have learned to see things, to come to the conclusion that one object is in a solid state while another is semi-fluid and another is liquid, is lastly an illusion of our perception that will resolve itself, once we have learned to see beyond the apparently obvious.

Scientific researchers are agreed that everything that

we perceive in this world consists of vibration, yet their extent, the resonance they elicit, the realms that are touched and influenced by them are only slowly being recognized and accepted.

Our thought processes and emotions, for instance, also contain powerful vibrations that cause specific effects. Animals and plants may react very directly to a loving or a rejecting attitude or feelings of fear. A dog that senses our fear of him is more apt to act aggressively. A plant in our house or garden that regularly receives our fond and admiring attention develops particularly well.

Gemstones cannot show us their reactions as directly as people, animals or plants can when they show their trust or confidence in us. That could lead us to assume at the outset, that we are dealing with lifeless matter. But stones vibrate on a different plane, send their messages via subtle energies that some mediumistically gifted persons can see, hear or both, but which we can feel, also, as through warmth, sudden perspiration or hot flashes, a prickling sensation, a rush of the blood, vibrating and states of trance.

The stones are simply there, and vibrate independent of objects or living beings. It is up to us to learn to assimilate these vibrations into our consciouness and to let their powers work in us. Thus they teach us essentials for our spiritual way: devotion and selfless love.

The simplest but also least conscious way of utilizing the gemstones, is to wear the stone we like and feel attracted to. Through their beauty and the fascination with which they literally attract us, a choice takes place that stimulates and supports something in us. There are good reasons for someone time and again admiring and chosing to wear a tiger-eye, someone else feeling drawn to jade, while someone else again would prefer to wear diamonds only, which may be completely contrary to another person's taste.

But the powers of the stones can also be implemented if we accept the teachings of old traditions and writings correlating gemstones with the signs of the Zodiac or with certain sicknesses. Yet, once we study these traditions more thoroughly we have to reach the conclusion that each school of thought has its own fundamental philosophy and direction, so that there is some common agreement but a great deal more divergence.

That is why I have chosen a form of working with gemstones that achieves its results through color vibrations and their resonances within us. This takes place in the subtly structured areas of our energy centers. The combination of energies from our power centers and the energies of the gemstones primarily provides our body and its subtler and coarser energy systems with purification and recharging. But through the energy centers the vibrations of the gemstones also reach our soul, whose densest vibrations we can find reflected in our state of mind and the way our emotions are expressed. In the same manner our spirit is stimulated, the densest vibrations of which we can determine in our thought patterns and the thoughts they emit, but which is also in touch with cosmic dimensions.

The messages of the stones that are being disseminated by this book are, however, also meant to serve the purpose of initiating an individual and increasingly intuitive approach to gemstones and their utilization.

Chapter II

Energy Centers
and Their Resonance
to the Colors of Stones

Energy centers are areas that transform energies from the cosmic space for the benefit of our body but also for all other dimensions of our being. These energies are always there, but in order to be utilized by us they must be brought to a certain oscillation that matches our being. This is why the centers are significant transformers and transmitters of the vitally important universal life-energy. But they are also places through which we can release energy that we have exhausted or which no longer corresponds to our requirements, and they retain information about various aspects of ourselves.

Everybody has these energy centers, even though they are not discernable to our usual way of seeing things. But there are people who have developed the ability to see these centers with all of their vibrations and colors. We may already feel the energy of the centers when we place gemstones on those parts of our bodies where the centers are located. The centers belong to the realm of subtle energies and processes that we can sense or see when we have become attuned to them.

The underlying principle resembles that of a transmitter and receiver. When both are tuned to the same frequency they are compatible, the receiver gets a clear message. A radio transmitter sends out waves of a certain length which are transformed into sound by the radio receiver, but only if the receiver has been activated. Television is another example of the same process. The broadcasting station sends out signals that pass through the atmosphere without being seen or heard, except by those with a corresponding receiver that has been activated.

The energy centers also work with certain frequencies, which are varied on many levels. They are attuned to information in form of color vibrations, and are therefore directly able to receive the color vibrations given off by gemstones. We possess seven major energy centers in various parts of the body, and secondary centers in the palms of our hands and soles of our feet. Each plays a certain role for body, mind and soul, and has a basic oscillation and a function corresponding to the color that is primarily connected to it. The color sequence is the same as that of the rainbow; the lowest energy center oscillates red, the uppermost oscillates violet.

With their vibrations the energy centers influence physical processes through the glands, but they also influence the meridians, the subtle energy pathways of the body. These are the densest vibrations. But they also penetrate all psychic areas, and with their most far-reaching vibrations the psyche itself and the emotions that we experience. Additionally they touch our mind, and here with their deepest oscillation our thinking and thought patterns. The highest and lightest vibrations reach our relations to the mental world and to the spirit beings, touch on forms and principles, our inner guide and our connection to our Higher Self.

Each energy center fulfills an individual function, for which there is a basic oscillation with a corresponding basic color, as well as one or more gemstones of the same hue.

For some energy centers additional stones have been cited that do not have the basic color, but yet fulfill the function of the center.

The Energy Centers

Survey of Significant Attributes

1. The Base Center
   Element: Earth
   Body part: Genital area
   Color: Red
   Stones: Jasper, agate, hematite, garnet, ruby

2. The Sacral Center
   Element: Water
   Body part: Abdomen, adrenal glands
   Color: Orange
   Stone: Carnelian

3. The Solar Plexus Center
   Element: Fire
   Body part: Belly, digestive tract
   Color: Yellow
   Stones: Yellow topaz, citrine, amber, yellow
   tigereye, rutile quartz, yellow tourmaline

4. The Heart Center
   Element: Earth, Water, Fire, Air
   Body part: Heart and surrounding area
   Color: Green and pink
   Stones: Chrysocolla, chrysoprase, chrysoberyl,
   chrysolite, moss agate, malachite, jade,
   emerald, calcite, tourmaline

5. The Throat Center
   Element: Air
   Body part: Below the larynx
   Color: Light blue
   Stones: Turquoise, chalcedony, blue topaz,
   aquamarine, fluorite, light and dark
   indicolite (blue tourmaline), pyrite,
   opal, moonstone, pearl

6. The Inner Eye Center
   Body part: Forehead
   Color: Dark blue
   Stones: Sodalite, blue tiger-eye, lapis lazuli,
   azurite, sapphire, rock crystal

7. The Crown Center
   Body part: Top of the head
   Color: Violet
   Stones: Amethyst, diamond

Hand Center
   Body part: Palms of the hands
   Stone: Rock crystal

Foot Center
   Body part: Center of soles of feet
   Stones: Snowflake obsidian, tourmaline quartz

The Base Center

The first energy center, located between the base of the spine and the pubic bone, has direct influence on our reproductive organs and sexual glands. On a physical level the center fulfills the task of regulating vital functions, such as the maintaining and renewing of the blood and cells. It thereby provides the body with elementary life force, coarse energy as is found in our bloodstream, for example.

Additionally, this center controls the basic energies essential for maintaining life, the sex drive, will-power and our life-force. These are fundamental necessities that can, however, turn into cravings such as unhealthy eating habits, alcoholism, smoking, drug addiction and others.

The Base Center programs our thinking in terms of patterns that primarily serve material-existential security and survival of the species, such as having a family and children, professional success, an adequate home of one's own, etc.

The vibrations within the Base Center are very dense and closely resemble those of the Earth. It oscillates in the base color red and resonates in the gemstones jasper, garnet, ruby, hematite and agate. Each of these stones in its own special way fulfills a basic function in maintaining life.

Jasper

Jasper is a fairly dense, opaque gemstone that comes in all earth hues: brown, green, reddish brown and sand-colored, which may also be found mixed in one stone. A very special variety is reddish brown jasper with hematite inclusions, which is particular beneficial for the maintainance of sound blood. Especially lovely is zebra-jasper found in Australia, named for its black and white bands, and landscape-jasper, also named for its appearance. Its structures are shaped like landscape contours or waves, and it is primarily found in subdued tones of beige, brown and grayish blue.

Despite its diverse nuances of color jasper belongs to the first and base energy center. It is a gemstone related to matter, that connects us with the elementary power of the Earth. Jasper is a valuable helper when a child is born, and is equally effective in the treatment of various illnesses of the uterus and Fallopian tubes, even if these are psychosomatic. Best for this purpose is red to reddish brown jasper that has been shaped and polished, fits the hand well and has a »soft«, almost supple feel to it.

Agate

Although red is not the agate's natural color, this instead being rather earthy and ranging from black and brown to dark shades of blue − often with crystal inclusions − it nonetheless belongs to the first energy center.

Since ancient times agates have been dyed by secret procedures and are therefore available in shades of intense red, orange, yellow, green and light blue.

For my work I prefer agates with natural coloring because of the purity of their vibrations. But artificially colored agates also have positive vibrations, which does not hold true for all gemstones treated in this manner. In accordance with their colors, dyed agates can be assigned other energy centers.

Agates are often marketed in slices or tumbler-polished. The latter term means that larger pieces of stone plus polishing material are put into a drum or tumbler, which then rotates for a given period of time. The forces of motion, the weight of the pieces themselves and the added material break up the stones and polish them. The results vary greatly in size and shape, are polished smooth and pleasant to the touch.

Agates let the love for our bodies grow stronger and support those organs involved in reproduction, especially if this part of the body is beset by problems or new life needs to be protected.

Slices of agate containing crystalline inclusions are of special significance for the processes of the first energy center. They protect new life, support the generation of cells and provide security. From the contours contained in the slice we can »read« what is taking place, which vibrations are being enhanced.

A crystalline inclusion usually has an oval shape, and thereby reminds us of an embryo safe and secure in the womb, surrounded as in the agate by black, brown or blue tones. Agate slices with such a configuration are well-suited for mothers-to-be, as the agate will transform the woman's fear of a new state or her worry about the health and welfare of the child into vibrations of confidence and loving expectation, and will enhance her feelings of joy.

As we were all once in a womb and while there gained first impressions that were an important influence on us, the agate will help us to cast off unconsciously retained, burdensome remnants of this phase.

Additionally, the agate will insure that we meet and are connected with loving people in our daily lives. In this context it will teach us knowledge of human nature that will sensitize our ability to differentiate between people that are truly for us and those wearing a smiling mask in order to deceive us.

Hematite

The surface of hematite shows a silvery metallic lustre while internally it is a deep shade of red. On the physical level hematite is very effective against anemia and other impairments of the blood and conditions of faintness. In times of recuperation following operations, illnesses and psycho-physical break-downs hematite will regenerate cells and blood and provide our bodies with a vigorous feeling of strength.

Garnet

Garnet is a deep red gemstone with subdued light reflection that supports the regeneration of the blood, but also the circulatory system. Its vibrations positively effect all of the levels of our being. It has invigorating influence on our sexual activities, and also supports our love of constructive work in the material world, as in the shaping of our home.

The garnet lets us enjoy being active, lends us drive, courage and spontaneous energy as well as confortable warmth.

Ruby

In the ruby a glinting deep shade of red is mixed with a radiant dark blue, so that this precious stone transmits a feeling of spirituality. Its vibration produces and supports the harmonious conjunction of physical and spiritual love. In the first energy center the ruby is the gemstone that puts us in touch with the higher ideals of love. It helps us to increasingly unfold and realize our soul-felt need for a unity of sexuality and spirituality with our partner. It promotes our desire for independence and freedom in love and partnership, and lets us find new forms of experience and expression.

But the ruby's vibrations also touch the Inner Eye Center and help us to fill our ideas and understanding with love and action, which furthers their growth and realization.

The Sacral Center

The second energy center is connected with the adrenal glands, with the excretory functions and the balance of flow in our body, but also with our relationships to others, how we establish contact with them, how we see ourselves and how we rest in ourselves. This center has the function of refining, of movement and activation, and it vibrates orange.

This is corresponded to by carnelian, which occurs in shades of light to deeply dark orange and is translucent to a degree.

Carnelian

At the physical level carnelian influences the organs involved in the excretory processes, but it also effects blood circulation and vascular congestion, and relieves varicose veins.

Carnelian always provides joyful, active vitality, and can therewith awaken new life energies and initiate creative processes. These vibrations enrich our feelings with creativity and sensuality. To the sex drive and survival instinct of the first energy center the second center now adds the sensual, erotic experience of love, and the imaginative and creative handling of one's environment. The carnelian lets these potentials vibrate stronger within the structure of our psyche, and thereby gain increased expression in our senses and our behavior.

On the mental plane our thoughts become filled with warmth, we refer increasingly to others, our frame of thought expands and we gain flexibility in everything.

The Solar Plexus Center

This energy center is the one best known in our culture. It is the Solar Plexus Center and has one central function as the center of exchange of physical and mental energies.

At the physical level it is connected with the pancreas and influences all of the digestive organs, the liver and the metabolism. This is where the alchemistic process of food transformation takes place, where the nourishment we ingest is broken down, changed and transmitted within the entire body in appropriate forms. But the energetical vibrations of our nourishment are also isolated and fed into the body's energy systems.

The third energy center also controls the vegetative nervous system, and contains the center of our emotional perception and expression. Through the solar plexus we register intellectually as well as intuitively, how others relate to us. Vice versa we also utilize this center to let others know how we appraise them. The solar plexus represents our Self, our individuality. Here we want to realize ourselves according to our ideals. That is why we are especially susceptible and vulnerable regarding vibrations in this area that could injure our ego. That's why in some cases we need to have a strong stomach.

The third energy center is ruled by the energy of the Sun: The will to consciously make use of all of the possibilities available to us − on a physical, mental and emotional plane. Here we can unfold and express strength and self-assurance. The solar plexus − well known through autogenous training − is our internal sun, our own center in which the forces of heaven and earth, matter and spirit, nourishment and breath, coarse and subtle energies join and influence each other, keep us alive and determine our attitude to life. Whether we are fearful and depressed, or act with joy, confidence and self-assurance is expressed through the vibrations of the solar plexus.

Here the base vibration is yellow and bright. The gemstones that belong to this center are yellow topaz, citrine, amber, yellow tiger-eye, rutile quartz and yellow tourmaline (ref. Heart Center).

Yellow Topaz

The yellow topaz reminds us of a glittering, golden stream of light and particularly influences our psyche. Its effect is that of a sun shining inside of us, melting away burdensome, obstructed feelings and dreary thoughts. The topaz fills us with warm, pleasing light and so much active power spreading out, that through a reversal of our mood we again devote ourselves to the joyful and vibrant aspects of life. It is especially helpful in counteracting depressions and anxiety.

During those times of the year when we have less sun and light reaching us, the topaz would be of benefit to everyone, as it can compensate for external darkness by providing internal light.

Citrine

While the citrine's vibrations primarily influence physical processes, they also affect the unfoldment of emotional and mental potential and its activation on the material plane – in other words, in our daily lives.

The citrine charges our metabolism with activity and stimulates the functions of the digestive tract. It can be of help in cases of repletion, stomach cramps and diabetes. Diabetics actually suffer from not being able to sufficiently express affection, and therefore often avail themselves of a substitute in eating too well, mostly too sweet. The citrine will not only help them physically by influencing the pancreas and therefore the production of insulin, but also on an emotional level by furthering the readiness and ability to manifest tenderness and share it with others. Through this the healing process is approached from its psychosomatical side and receives intensive support.

Where the activation of latently present inherent capabilities and powers is called for, citrine crystal points are best. Citrine originated through amethysts being subjected to intense heat, and is therefore a gemstone possessing double transforming powers. The violet amethyst puts us in touch with the mental world, which makes it a stone for meditation and transformation. When the fire is added again – always a very powerful, purifying and changing effect – another transformation takes place. This is radiated as vibration by the citrine and helps us to translate impressions and realizations, but also intuitive perceptions, cognitively and actively into our daily environment.

Citrines that still possess their crystal parts, be it below the natural crystal point or after tumbler-polishing, are always of help in clarifying or shedding light on a matter, or in letting a rudimentary ability develop in such a way or enter consciousness, so that it can become a living part of our personality.

Amber

Amber is a very light »stone« that actually is not a stone at all, as it originated in the vegetable kingdom. Amber is fossilized resin and often contains inclusions of insects or bits of plants. Its color ranges from pale yellow to shades of honey and a rich brown, and it may be brightly translucent to opaque. Its lightness tends to surprise us, its warm sheen makes us optimistic, and its inclusions fascinate and please us. With these »gifts« amber helps us primarily to advance in the material world. All of its vibrations are related to matter, so that amber brings good fortune, success and gains on all material levels:
- in relation to and connection with people, whether in one's own family or with colleagues and business partners;
- in professional matters and business decisions;
- in creating and maintaining one's own home ...

The amber's sun energy shows us how we can realize ourselves in our life: It teaches us to reach the right decisions and to handle all of life's situations skilfully, and brings us into contact with people that support our development.

Yellow Tiger-eye

The tiger-eye shimmers in shades of yellow and brown. It appears to be alive, because as we turn it, its appearance and gleam change. It makes wishes for warmth and comfort come true, yet also refines our thinking where it concerns itself with material questions. Where this way of thinking is already established the tiger-eye will enhance it, so that someone who is mentally one-sidedly occupied with himself and his environment will find the powers of the tiger-eye leading him to the limits of his intellectual abilities to comprehend, and will then have to learn to permit a different and expanded frame of experience to enter his life.

Rutile Quartz

Rutile quartz is a gemstone of healing and harmony. It is a clear crystal with inclusions of golden thread-like crystals of rutile, a titanium mineral. These inclusions have changed the vibrations of the crystal considerably. Instead of rejecting the material foreign to itself, it integrated it into its being. In this it differs from all other crystals. It contains the vibrations of this union and therefore of uplifting in it, a state accompanied by a special kind of power for healing and harmonizing.

On the physical level rutile quartz teaches the cells and their consciousness by example to again attain harmonious and strong and therefore healthy vibration. It can be placed on any ill or painful part of the body and will have a harmonizing effect.

Additionally it gives off large amounts of golden light that permits our psyche and emotions to enter a warm and pleasant state.

In the spiritual world rutile quartz puts us in touch with the angels of light and their wise and loving guidance, and protects us from burdensome, aggressive energies on this level.

During the day it is best to carry rutile quartz in one's pocket so that its vibrations can exercise their strongest influence on the lower three energy centers. If we place it under our pillow at night, it will calm our thoughts, guard our sleep and the journeys of our soul into other realms.

If one has difficulty breathing it is best to wear rutile

quartz as a pendant on a chain around the neck; in case of pain in the area of the heart, a longer chain will help place the stone effectively. The same applies, should asthma, bronchitis or tuberculosis be the problem. If there is difficulty swallowing, a cough, a cold or a thyroid condition, the stone should be worn directly on the neck, but for maximum effect in form of a chain of the stones linked together.

The three lower energy centers that we have dealt with so far primarily serve to satisfy our existential needs in the material world, and are meant to establish a harmonious foundation for our spiritual unfoldment and development, which receive stronger emphasis in the following energy centers.

The Heart Center

The location of the fourth energy center is the heart and its vicinity. It therefore influences all of the vital functions connected with the heart, and is related to the thymus and the immune system.

In order to master this task over a lifetime, pulsing, life sustaining, regenerative and transforming powers are needed. These vibrations are emitted by green gemstones possessing the color of nature — of the meadows, forests and the entire vegetable kingdom.

But the heart is also the place where emotions are dealt with, the place of purification, of harmony, of love for all and of peace. We can take someone »into our heart« and not mean the personified love for that individual, but rather a love that is far more comprehensive, that embraces all of creation with its animals, plants, stones, natural features and wonders.

And in this area the green gemstones are helpful, too. They teach us to discover beauty, to respect it and creatively bring it forth ourselves — be it in the feelings we project, in our home, our garden or in whichever area that suits our inclinations. Green gemstones stimulate us to experience love, joy and fulfillment in all that we do, but also to give more love of ourselves.

In the world of stones we find the green vibrations in chrysocolla, chrysoprase, chrysoberyl, chrysolite, moss agate, malachite, emerald, calcite, tourmaline and jade.

As the first of the energy centers so far discussed, the Heart Center is also connected to a higher dimension, to the vibrations of selfless love, of Christian love, of love for one's neighbor. This kind of love is no longer tied down by egocentric human wishes and demands, or one's own conceptions and expectations, nor to reciprocation of emotions. It flows, pours itself out and simply gives itself, and no longer asks for a reward, does not evaluate or judge. At issue here are the fundamental prerequisites for our spiritual growth.

The pink gemstones with their delicate, gentle vibrations also belong to this realm. They open our heart for love that is higher, subtler and more spiritual, and thereby lead us to new and broader values and goals.

Rubellite (pink tourmaline), rhodonite, rhodochrosite, rose quartz, kunzite and coral vibrate on this plane.

Green Gemstones
Chrysocolla

The chrysocolla is an opaque stone containing various bright tones of green and blue as well as black. When the blue tones dominate it resembles tourquoise. However, it is much »softer«, more porous and somewhat »wilder« in appearance than tourquoise. The chrysocoll has very strong vibrations of love of nature in it and helps us to treat our own body and its needs lovingly and respectfully, but also to do the same with our environment, with all of nature and the nourishment and strength it provides us.

It increases the wish to live healthier and more naturally, and teaches us to recognize the beauty of nature. More than ever before the Earth today needs our loving attention and respect for the natural laws and cycles.

But as we can only give what we have integrated into our being, creation has wisely provided a stone that will let love for ourselves and for nature grow and deepen within us in close interaction.

With its basic vibration the chrysocolla always leads us to love of nature, teaches us to develop qualities and perceptions through admiration and appreciation of a flower, fruit, garden, tree or forest. Qualities that are important for our well-being and our overall development on the physical, emotional, intellectual and spiritual plane, such as gratitude, joy and wonder.

Chrysoprase

Unlike the chrysocolla, the chrysoprase contains powers of light that refine and elevate its vibrations. It radiates a gentle light green and teaches us to recognize the light and beauty in all plants. Also, it puts us in touch with the spiritual aspects of plants, which supports our approach to nature on a subtle plane. It relates strongly to all fruit trees, and brings us the stength and wisdom of full bloom, ripening and letting go, just as trees flower, develop their fruit until it is fully ripe and then release it. Especially in difficult times of our life this natural cycle can help us to gain far-reaching understanding, to realize deep inside ourselves how the processes of being born and dying function in us, in nature and in all of creation. The chrysoprase's soft light gives us confidence and serenity as prerequisites that make these realizations possible for us.

Chrysoberyl

Chrysoberyl is found in tones ranging from yellow, honey-colored and bright brown to pale and olive green. For the Heart Center the green varieties are important. Despite their color they also contain the vibrations of honey-yellow and brown, so that they reach the Solar Plexus Center in order to provide the organs of the area with warmth, harmony and relaxation. Chrysoberyl helps us to deal with emotions lovingly and with understanding, and its gentle warmth dissolves hardness in ourselves and in our dealings with others. It connects »heart« and »abdomen« and lets us live more attentively and warm-heartedly.

Chrysolite (Peridot)

The Peridot has a great deal of sunlight and radiance in it and puts us in contact with the vegetable kingdom, similar to the chrysoprase. Its radiation, however, is more active and instills warmth, vitality and cheerfulness in our feelings.

Its vibrations should be applied where emotional coldness manifests itself with all of its possible physical effects, such as frigidity, gout, rheumatism, arthritis, arthrosis or diseases of the coronary vessels, where behavioral effects are evident, as in exaggerated vulnerability, lack of confidence or callousness, or where thought patterns are affected, as shown by destructive thinking, self-pity or arrogance.

Moss Agate

Moss agate seals our love of nature, of creativity, caring and cultivating. It teaches us to talk to plants, to find out when and where they want to be planted, how and when harvested, watered, fertilized and cared for, what fits in which company, and which cosmic rhythms (forces and cycles of the moon) affect them.

In the process a number of benefits occur on several levels. Firstly, plants can grow and develop in their natural, optimal time frames and in the proper environment. Secondly, we learn to re-establish our life in harmony with nature by observing and recognizing these processes. And the knowledge that we gain we will rediscover in other areas of our lives, and thereby learn to listen to and observe subtle inner relationships. Our senses, that have become used to being directed towards the external world through education and habit, will thusly be sensitized for subtle life systems and the way they achieve effects.

Malachite

Malachite is a green, opaque stone striped with dark green bands or circles and spiraling patterns. Its light and dark shades of green put us in touch with the polarity of the power of love. Its patterns bring us in contact with fundamental energy forms of life, with mobility, liveliness, order, vitality, joy, security and their possible obstructions.

The malachite is a stone of compassion. Through it our love for others is stimulated and strengthened. The malachite helps us to develop understanding and patience toward our own weaknesses and errors. Through this we also learn to be more tolerant and loving to people around us. For our own difficulties we no longer shift the responsibility to our environment, partner, children, relatives, colleagues, superiors or politicians. Instead we recognize that feeling sick, miserable, tired, irritated or angry is a consequence of our own behavior, and how we can change that.

On the emotional plane the vibrations of malachite teach us to relax and set reactions of love for ourselves in motion. On the mental plane they lead us to think positively and, if necessary, accelerate a change in our attitude towards ourselves and others.

Such changes soon effect relaxation throughout the body and are of great help particularly in treating painful conditions of the heart, provided the pain originated through our tendency to reject or perhaps even fight people near us.

Jade

Jade is found in a variety of colors: white, yellow, green, pink, brown, violet and black. The best know variety is green, which has a special relationship to the Heart Center.

Jade radiates the attributes of renewal and strengthening of the bonds of love. How this happens depends to a large degree on the state of development of the person resounding to these vibrations and supporting them.

Traditionally, a certain awe and reverence have been connected with jade, as well as the discovery and experience of beauty in all things.

On the emotional plane jade brings peace, harmony and a quiet joy up from the depths of the soul, connects these with our mental world and also lets our body relax and become tranquil and satisfied. It is a pleasure to practise autogenous training or other relaxing exercises in conjunction with this stone, to meditate with it or just to put it under the pillow and thus carry it over into sleep. Children that sleep restlessly or are plagued by frightening dreams can be helped in this manner. If the children are small, the stone should be sown into a soft pillow.

Emerald

The emerald is a radiant, dark green gemstone whose entire effect is marked by clarity and beauty. It is the stone of all-encompassing love.

It permeates all of our love with this power, challenges us with its directness and intensity, so that we may equal its shining, powerful radiance. It purifies our feelings of love for the Earth and all of its creatures and lets us bloom internally. It puts us in touch with everything obstructing these radiant vibrations, so that we can learn to perfect our love repeatedly in different situations.

Using the emerald we can bring a great deal of healing energy for the regeneration of nature to Earth from the cosmic realm.

When we meditate, we hold the emerald in our hand or place it on our heart. With our powers of imagination and empathy we then travel to plants, trees, forests, meadows and fields, see and feel how the green rays of the emerald grow so great and bright, that they pervade the entire scene in our vision. We see, for instance, the forest we imagine being illuminated from the ground upward by the magnificent, pure green of the emerald. This scene we study for awhile with our inner eye.

Calcite

Calcite is a generally colorless stone that does occur in very pale green and has a somewhat watery translucence. It forms the bridge to the pink stones and therewith to selfless love, as it just barely vibrates green and with its light brings us close to the basic vibration of the pink stones. Calcite is a rather crystalline stone that feels »soft« despite its edges, and is not suitable for polishing. Through it we establish contact with nature in the spiritual sense. Calcite only contains a very slight, subtle connection to the power of the vegetable kingdom and teaches us to turn the love that we have learned to develop and express on the material plane away from the object (plant, animal, stone, person) and towards the higher, spiritual forms and being in creation. With its softly green crystal light it leads us gently higher and helps us to find our way to the spiritual world. It always supports our yearning for spiritual connection, our self-communion and our need for harmony.

On the physical plane calcite counteracts processes of sedimentation and hardening and has positive influence on all illnesses of bones, such as rigidity of joints, fractures or the remnants of older fractures and calcification.

Tourmaline

Tourmaline occurs in all colors of the spectrum and can produce a variety of shades and hues of its own. Often a stone will show two or more colors, and it gives off a gentle light. Tourmaline always enables us to find a way out of life situations or behavioral patterns that make us feel restricted, confined, in a dead-end street or even totally exhausted. The stone's individual color determines, which energy center will be especially reached.

Shades of light yellow to brown, for example, belong to the Navel Center, and are effective in all hopeless situations having to do with the connections and functions of the third center, such as illnesses of the stomach or digestive tract, depressions, anxiety, difficulties in realizing creative spiritual powers, feelings of inferiority and bleak thoughts.

Green tourmaline opens doors via the Heart Center. With its help we can free ourselves, find ways out of difficulties in love. It supports us in eliminating obstructions in our treatment of ourselves and people to whom we feel connected.

Green and pink tourmaline is very special. It unites the vibrations of love in the Heart Center: green — love on the material plane, and pink — selfless love. Green and pink tourmaline will help us to integrate these two forms of love, but will also protect the delicate vibrations of higher, selfless love from other influences of our being that are not yet equally selfless. This takes place particularly with cross-section slabs of tourmaline that have pink centers edged with green.

Pink Stones
Pink Tourmaline

If a tourmaline is pink it helps us to manifest a deep spiritual desire for selfless love together with a partner. The tourmaline frees us from old patterns and shows us new ways of meeting in interpersonal relationships that include the spiritual powers and teach them to unfold.

Rhodonite

In rhodonite pink and black are combined – the pink representing subtle, elevated, selfless love, and the black, matter, Earth, everyday life. In this way the stone makes it possible for us to include selfless love in life on Earth, to integrate it firmly into our daily life as well as our private and professional sphere of action.

As rhodonite is a stone of action, we can implement many changes and initiate processes of renewal with its help, but not, as in the case of the emerald, in quiet meditation, but instead by acting. Rhodonite is opaque, and therefore vibrates differently than the translucent emerald does. It gives us the strength and motivation to fill our environment with love in our daily work as well as in our meeting with people.

Rhodochrosite

Rhodochrosite keeps us in motion. Its basic pink is often streaked with white wave-like patterns that suggest energy and movement and let us associate a connection to water and the soul. Rhodochrosite keeps the subtlest energy channels in our body open, but also lets us continue to yearn for more fulfillment through selfless love and the meeting with the divine in ourselves. In that its power constantly re-activates this spiritual need in us, our love and ability to love is guided to higher dimensions of our being.

Rhodochrosite crystals of a deep pink color are also found. They guide us to a purification of our emotional life and a clear alignment of our life in the sense of selfless love and serving for the benefit of the Earth and all of its creatures.

Coral

The colors of the best-known corals range from white, white spotted with pale pink, pink, salmon-pink to dark red.

Corals grow organically, singly and as parts of coral reefs, and bear in them the qualities of the ocean — depth, silence, perseverance, movement, beauty, purity and the life-giving — and bring them, accented by their respective colors, into our being through the Heart Center.

White coral cleanses our thinking of everything burdensome, dark and confused, and thereby lets us feel relief.

White coral spotted with pale pink cleanses our soul of lowly inclinations and feelings such as envy, jealousy, greed, slander and contempt. With its help all of these feelings and thoughts will be replaced with gentility and harmony.

Pink coral lets our heart share in the »jubilation of the heavenly host« and enables us to absolve our daily tasks with pleasure.

Salmon-pink coral enhances our blood circulation, the regeneration of blood cells, the removal waste as well as the cleansing of the kidneys. Here is a connection with the second energy center.

Dark red coral strengthens our heart physically, and is therefore related to the first energy center.

Rose Quartz

Pale pink, translucent rose quartz possesses very subtle vibrations that always call forth and strengthen something about to begin — just like a rose-bud is already complete, yet needs time and energy to blossom and unfold its full beauty. Rose quartz enables our delicate, very vulnerable feelings to express themselves more strongly, and it teaches us that we do not have to don protective armor or erect a wall of defensive, rejectory and harsh emotions to safeguard them. This stone encourages us to show and live the gentle, soft and lovely, but also to respect these feelings in others. On our way to spiritual unfoldment, healing and compassion it can also be a good companion and protector.

Kunzite

Kunzite unites pink and pale violet in a very clear, transparent stone. Thus it brings the vibrations of higher love from the Heart Center into unison with the violet of the Crown Center. The selfless love is pervaded by the spirit of the mental world, which bears in it the voiding of the »I-you separation« and thereby strongly supports the basic function of pink gemstones, while at the same time raising it due to the high energy standard of the seventh center. Owing to its fibrous longitudinal growth the kunzite also enhances directness of thinking and feeling in us, as well as an upward striving of the powers of selfless love in order to perfect the divine within us.

The Throat Center

This energy center is located in the area of the larynx and regulates self-expression. It influences the thyroid gland and its important functions in the metabolism, the quality of body tissues, the structure of the bones and the entire nervous system. The functioning of the thyroid gland determines whether we are mentally and physically lethargic or mobile, whether we are weary and sad or energetic and cheerful, whether we are nervous or tranquil. It therefore has fundamental effects on our entire well-being.

But the Throat Center is also the area that governs our ability to express ourself with our voice, our communication with the environment in the broadest sense of the term.

Our voice, which is to say how we speak and also what we say — and the force and emphasis that accompany our words — are regulated by this center.

The fifth energy center has a direct channel to higher spiritual planes, and by means of our speech and personality helps these subtle energies find expression. It determines the effect we have on others and provides our creative forces with the necessary means of expression.

In this center the color light blue vibrates, the color of the sky and the seas. Here infinity is reflected, the sea reminding us of the unfathomed depths of our soul, and the sky of the endless vastness and transparency of our spirit.

Light blue provides the body, and particularly the nervous system, with tranquility and relaxation, gives our restless thoughts quiet and calmness, and our soul the peace and serenity it needs in order to draw resources from out of the depths and to unite with the divine vibrations.

All light blue stones belong to this center: turquoise, chalcedony, blue topaz, aquamarin, fluorite, light and dark blue tourmaline. But also pyrite, opal, moonstone and pearl fulfill functions that correspond to this energy center, often in conjunction with the Heart Center.

Turquoise

The most sought after variety of this opaque stone is radiant light blue; the green shades are less popular. It protects the energy field that surrounds our body from being burdened with vibrations stemming from the spiritual world, and supports constructive energies giving strength and power coming at us from the cosmos. These could, however, be powers originating in the world of nature spirits.

Turquoise is a strong protective shield. By its intense blue radiation it wards off undesired »visits« from spiritual worlds, curses, black magic and similar threats.

Turquoise will protect a speaker from attacks and lend his words additional power. For this the stone should be worn at the neck or held in the hand.

Turquoise adds the pure beauty of spiritual depths into our self-expression, and awakens or supports our sense of beauty and the wish to expand beauty on this Earth.

Chalcedony

A bright, translucent type of chalcedony is available ground and polished to cabochon-shape, and a denser, opaque variety can be had tumbler-polished.

The gentle light of the cabochon brings peace and tranquility to our mind and is a balm for worn nerves and disturbing thoughts.

The opaque chalcedony shows wave-like markings and strongly reminds us of the movement and power of the sea, and sometimes of white clouds against a light blue sky. Accordingly, this gemstone adds movement to our self-expression, enhances the flow of speech and lends voice and gestures smoothness, vitality and inner power as well as concentrated inspiration stemming from the spirit of life.

Cahlcedony is considered the stone of speakers, and it assists all who have to prepare or give a speech or express themselves verbally for other purposes in the drafting of lectures, papers and dissertations, scientific presentations, letters and contracts.

The opaque chalcedony also has beneficial influence on the function of the thyroid gland, as it regulates the metabolic rate.

Blue Topaz

The light blue topaz is very similar to aquamarine. With its gentle vibrations it consistently helps us to practically sweep away entrenched patterns of feeling, thinking and acting that we would like to process and let go of. Therefore it helps us in situations in which we experience physical pain, emotional suffering and/or clinging to an opinion, an object or a person, or the refusal to accept certain life events, and leads us out of the state of anxiety to a solution and relief.

Aquamarine

The aquamarine is a transparent, brightly radiant stone that reminds us of the lightness of air and the blue of the sky. It puts us in touch with the spiritual world, its light-beings and the divine power of healing, and causes our Throat Center to radiate.

Its effect calms irritations of the air passages and mucous membranes and, in conjunction with a green stone, helps in cases of asthma, whooping cough and diphtheria.

We can meditate well with the aquamarine if we want to be a pure channel of divine love. But it also helps us when we turn depressive because of overcast skies, suffer changes of weather or headaches that may or may not be connected to this.

In order to meditate we assume a comfortable position, place the aquamarine on the neck or the forehead, close our eyes and travel in our imagination to a beautiful place in a meadow, on a mountain, under palm trees or by a seashore, allow the beauty and stillness of the nature around us to sink in, and observe the clear light blue of a sunny sky. While this is happening the aquamarine pervades and intensifies the blue with its radiating vibrations.

Fluorite

Fluorite grows in crystals, which, when struck correctly, break down into octahedrons. The fluorite then has the shape of two pyramids joined base to base. Its colors are milky white, yellow, green, light blue and light to very dark violet. As the double pyramid shape is the fluorite's natural form, it contains the energy patterns and powers of the pyramid and transmits these to our being.

A reflection of this is the energy field of our body. The lower point of the octahedron is located in our Base Center. From there the energy flow spirals upward to the level of our shoulders and the Throat Center. At this point its greatest expansion and the transformation of forces take place. Rising further, the

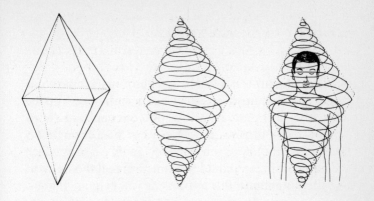

energy spiral concentrates up to the peak of the octahedron slightly above the Crown Center.

The spiral pattern is consistently repeated in subtle energy fields, but it also manifests itself in more material forms such as snail-shells and seashells; it is a fundamental pattern of life energy.

Fluorite brings fulfillment and abundance, forgiveness and blessing into our entire being and to our actions, and lets us enter into a strong conjunction with high-frequency cosmic energies. These help us on the way to awareness to accept responsibility for all of our thoughts, feelings and actions, and so to grow closer to our holistic, divine nature. Fluorite supports and satisfies our desire for spiritual connection and our own perfection, as well as life on Earth in divine wisdom and love in all aspects.

Fluorite teaches us spiritual unity with all of creation, inspires our spirit with divine law and insures their realization and proliferation.

Light and Dark Blue Tourmaline

A tourmaline that ranges from light to dark blue color nuances helps in the case of energies blocked in the Throat Center that are involved in our spiritual development. It confronts us with psychic pain brought on by the inadequacy of our conduct. In all cases in which we know what we should be doing but feel too weak to meet this standard, this tourmaline will help us. It lends us the strength to solve recurring situations of this type. (Ref. also tourmaline in the Heart Center).

Pyrite

With its golden sheen pyrite is connected with a higher energy field that will help us to solve problems in a particularly powerful way when the time is right or our development permits it.

This principle is applicable on all levels. It is possible, for example, to heal chronic pain or a chronic illness, as soon as we have learned the lesson the illness or pain is trying to teach us, and then need the strength to implement the necessary changes in our life.

In order to be able to fully assimilate the pyrite's helpful, energetic vibrations, we must in a sense have reached our limits, must accept in our innermost being that a re-orientation is at hand. Because only then will a process of realization — coupled with divine love and wisdom — set in, that can release powerful transforming forces, intensify our powers of perception and refine our means of expression.

Opal

Opals are available in the most iridescent of colors that sparkle in myriad forms of expression. They stimulate effervescence and variety in our lives. Not everyone is capable of realizing this much diversity in one life, and could be overtaxed by the opal's energy.

Opals with a light blue primary color available as so-called platelets have the gentlest vibrations. A thin opal slice or plate is mounted on a dark base, usually obsidian or agate dyed black, or a light ceramic base, and its upper surface is protected by a plate of glass or crystal. These processed opals are inexpensive, but their vibrations are altered somewhat due to their connection with other minerals and materials like ceramic, glass and adhesive. Yet they still retain the opal's strong vibrations.

Blue opals stimulate gentle natures and help manifest livelier, many-sided forms of expression.

Opals with shades of blue and green on a brown base supply everyday life with new inspiration and energy.

Opals with shades of green and red on a brown base

stimulate a variety of forms of expression and dynamic action on the material plane.

Opals with tones of blue and green support new impulses on the mental level.

Blue and green opals spotted with yellow, orange and red activate blood circulation and call forth an energetic attitude to life full of sparkling joy.

As varied as the coloring and splendor of the opals is their range of effects and vibrations, which for this reason can be circumscribed at best.

White opals are very special. Their base of white is seeded with luminescent dots of colored light that come to life when the stone is moved. They effect purification in many areas and levels of our behavior and stimulate powers that bring us closer to our own souls and the perfection of our feelings of love.

The bright orange shining fire opal also has a special position. It rarely opalesces as it usually lacks the iridescent point of light. For this reason it is facetted to bring out its fire.

The fire opal arouses expressions of higher spiritual love and with its effects also touches on the Heart Center. Its strong fiery vibrations support the power in us to awaken universal love in the hearts of others and strengthens the feeling of being one with God.

Moonstone

The best-known moonstone is milky white, pale yellow, pink or translucent and has a subtle royal blue sheen to it. Its gentle, unobtrusive yet profound light, usually not fully appreciable until the stone is turned back and forth, connects us to the female principle, the soft and tender, but also with our intuition. It helps young girls to unfold their femininity and to cast off inhibitions in the expression of their womanhood. The moonstone's vibrations also have very favorable effects on women who tend to appear boyish or masculine: they establish better contact with their female nature. Men who are willing to explore their own female energy better and to manifest their conduct will be supported in this by the moonstone.

This gemstone possesses a certain mysterious fascination and attraction, as well as a pleasant, supple mobility. These qualities it also awakens in us.

Pearl

The pearl contains the power and purity of the seas. When we surround ourselves with the vibrations of the pearl we encounter people and situations that require that we learn by experience to infuse our emotions and thoughts with pure clarity. With these vibrations the pearl also influences our Heart Center.

The purification of our emotional and mental worlds is often related to a confrontation with memories of pain and anguish. This may be why traditionally pearls are said to be connected with tears. But the pearl's vibrations always provide us with the chance to settle with old experiences deemed forgotten and with painful impressions and hurts, and to integrate these into our conscious Self.

But pearls also protect us from dangers and envelop us with wisdom and serenity, for which purpose it is best to wear them as a closed string around the neck. But some people may consider a string of pearls so worn constrictive or even regard it as a constraining chain. It depends very much on individual nature, on the state of development of the conscious mind and how these factors express themselves in patterns of perception and thinking.

On the physical plane pearls work supportively with the powers of the sea and stimulate excretory processes and purification.

Because of its mode of origin the pearl teaches us acceptance and integration of characteristics that seem foreign to us and which we may not wish to acknowledge. A mollusk surrounds a grain of sand or other foreign matter with mother-of-pearl and is thereby protected from injury by the intruder, yet at the same time has made it a part of itself. The pearl therefore transmits a feeling of acceptance and security.

Inner Eye Center

The sixth center is located in the forehead area. It is the seat of intuition and inspiration, of introspection, clairvoyance and extrasensory hearing, of heeding the inner voice. This energy center is connected to the pituitary gland, which regulates the functions of all other glands and is therefore the control and exchange center between body and spirit.

Principles, divine wisdom, the unfolding of higher consciousness, spiritual healing, holy law, faith, trust, the divine light within the soul and the devout recognition, comprehension and application of these powers are all inherent to the Inner Eye Center.

It is stimulated by the color blue, through sodalite, lapis lazuli, azurite and sapphire. In connection with the Navel Center the blue tiger-eye also belongs here, as does rock crystal. (Ref. to description of the hand energy centers).

Sodalite

Sodalite, a dark blue opaque stone sometimes striped with white or orange bands, supports our loyalty to ourselves, our world view, our principles of life and higher goals. Of the dark blue stones also known as »sacred stones«, it is the most strongly related to the material world.

That is why the sodalite directs the forces of trust and faith towards earthly processes. It spurs us on to realize our ideals and goals in daily life. Additionally, it lends us the power to stand up for our convictions. In this manner it increases our self-confidence and makes us resolute. Sodalite calms and strengthens our nerves and lets our trust in inner, higher guidance grow.

Blue Tiger-Eye

The difference between this and other tiger-eyes is a blue sheen that can range to blue-black. It pervades matter with spirit and teaches us to see the inner structure of the body and its energy movements — for example the skeletal frame, joints, organs, blood vessels, lymphatic ducts, meridians, etc. The tiger-eye enhances our optical vision, so that we see more clearly inside and outside of ourselves, and we learn to recognize the things in our life that we would rather not behold, things that we have been »protecting« ourselves from. But as the tiger-eye also contains gradations of yellow and brown, it helps us to implement our realizations in daily life and stabilize our ego through vibrations from the Navel Center. This also provides us with more flexibility in regard to philosophical concepts and opinions of others, which increases our compassion and tolerance.

Lapis Lazuli

Lapis lazuli is a »sacred stone«, a meditation stone of the most splendid deep blue, but often streaked with grey, which enormously reduces its spiritual as well as material worth. Entire altars and even tempels were inlaid with it. It connects us with whatever is sacred to us, that which we adore and revere. It enhances our introspection, our pretersensual capabilities, our trust in higher, divine guidance as well as our ability to believe and strength of faith, and gives us the feeling of being secure in the cosmos, our true home.

We often find golden pyrite inclusions in lapis lazuli that remind us of the starry sky. This establishes a resonance to the light of the stars and other planets.

Without the use of additional stones we may also employ lapis lazuli on other energy centers in meditation. We place it on the Inner Eye Center, visualize our union with the star-studded firmament und permit ourselves to be touched by the great silence and peace in God.

We should, however, refrain from letting lapis lazuli accompany us in sleep. because it can move us into dimensions of space that our perceiving consciousness cannot decode or integrate into the Here and Now, which can only lead to disorientation.

Azurite

Azurite is a mineral of a beautiful royal blue color that occurs as crystals having a vitreous lustre, but also in an amorphous form or as small spheres often times growing on malachite, so that the blue is coupled with green. It opens the door to spiritual connections and growth, but also for an expansion of consciousness for Mankind as a whole. It increases our compassion for others as well as the pervasion of the intellect with love and respect. Beyond that it supports our concentration and ability to absorb information. This is beneficial on the material plane by enabling us to solve problems better that require a high degree of concentration when we wear an azurite or have it near us at our place of work.

But it is also the stone that supports our willingness and ability to meditate and stimulates our preternatural potential. It has very high and beautiful vibrations.

In its spherical form, which is often split in two so that a deep blue shining crystal »star« becomes visible at its core, the azurite lets us discover our dual soul, which we seek here on Earth as the optimum augmentation of our being.

Sapphire

The sapphire radiates in the loveliest shades of blue — from a clear light blue to cornflower blue to royal blue and deeper shades — but also in all of the other colors of the spectrum, whose vibrations are also contained in the blue sapphires we know. Therefore all areas and dimensions of our being are touched by its radiance, which fortifies faith and trust.

It is a stone of spiritual purification and renewal. More than any other blue stone it support the strength of our faith, but demands steadfastness on our part so that we do not deviate from the life mission our soul has chosen for itself. With its deep, radiant power it leads us to the realization of higher ideals and goals. This leads to our repeatedly being confronted by particularly those aspects of our behavior that obstruct this, caused by a disproportionately strong ego.

The sapphire teaches us that there is a greater power than our own desire and will, and that we are unburdened and strengthened when we enter into closer union with this divine power and align our actions according to the flow of divine love and not counter to it.

The sapphire is a stone with a mighty radiation, and because of the great challenge it represents it cannot be worn by everyone.

Its light lets us perceive never-ending divine love particularly in times of illness, need and distress, whereby we receive the opportunity to implement basic changes, for which we would not see the necessity under other circumstances. In overcoming these ills permanent well-being, growth and expansion of consciousness can take place if we experience the divine power and make it a part of our fundamental motivation, our entire life.

And that is the reason why our soul has come here, to Earth, into an existence bound to a physical body: to accept the challenge of certain particular experiences.

Rock Crystal

Rock crystal is the Bringer of Light. Its designation »crystal« already speaks of the power of »Christ in all«. Through this energy center it particularly helps us to gain contact with the energy field of the spirit of Christ, leads us to the divine light in our soul and to a conscious, strong and radiant union with our Higher Self.

It purifies and clears our thoughts and ideas and puts us in touch with divine wisdom, strength of faith and intuitive experience. (Refer also to the description of rock crystal given under the chapter on Hand Energy Centers).

The Crown Center

This center, located at the very top of the head, connects us with the highest cosmic energies and serves our expansion of consciousness for the purpose of our conscious fusion with the cosmos. Parallel to this the realization takes place, that all is one. Our own body and life are still seen individually, but no longer separated from those of others, but rather as components of an all-encompassing creation.

If this energy center is open wide, a reversal of the radiation takes place. Not only are spiritual energies of the highest plane received then, but also a shower of golden light and shining rays of sunlight. This state is symbolized iconographically by a halo, and it is a sign of of the manifestation of divinity, of enlightenment, the experiencing of Christ and of the highest wisdom.

In the body this center relates to the pineal gland beneath the brainstem, whose function is not fully known yet. What is known is that it influences growing processes.

Spiritual healing, which takes place in the sense of one being a channel for divine love, the universal life-force, is nurtured by the »higher« cosmic energies that reach us through the Crown Center.

The base color of this center is violet. In the world of gemstones this corresponds to the amethyst, whose color ranges from a pale pink-violet to lilac and deep violet shades. The violet fluorides belong here (refer to the Throat Center), but also the diamond with its pure and perfect light.

Amethyst

The amethyst connects us with the spiritual world and power of our thoughts. It opens our mind to new ideas, intuition and inspiration and lends us the strength to mentally solve problems facing us, including the field of research. Inventions and sudden cognitive flashes are supported by the amethyst on the lowest and densest plane of thinking dealing with the material world.

Particularly Pisces are helped by the amethyst to apply some of their strong, sensitive nature and intuitive abilities to everyday life on the material plane, so that they will grow more closely connected to the Earth and reality.

For those born under all other signs of the zodiac the vibrations of the amethyst effect the exact opposite. It leads them away from dense matter and into the subtle spiritual and mental processes of life, and shows them the way to higher forms of existence, opening the way to other dimensions of being.

The amethyst leads us to the place that corresponds with our inner calling, there, where we can best grow in accordance with our capabilities. The spiritual qualities which the amethyst awakens in us and permits us to radiate are compassion and wisdom.

Because it transforms coarse vibrations from the realm of higher consciousness into more subtle frequencies, the amethyst is a stone of great importance for the Earth and its further development. It transforms and increases all of the energies in our bodies, our mental and spiritual being and in all of the beings on this Earth, so that an increasingly holistic and universal consciousness is created. This is one reason, why today amethysts are found in large numbers and are therefore increasingly affordable: so that its powers will manifest themselves in order to help the Earth and its inhabitants reach a new consciousness. As late as the Middle Ages it was still very rare and was treasured like a diamond. It was considered very precious and was highly prized by ecclesiastical and secular dignitaries. The amethyst's vibrations can vary greatly, depending on whether it is a fully developed crystal, a crystal pyramid, tumbler-polished, or cut and polished to other shapes, and if it is trasparent or opaque. We should choose a stone that relates to us, be it because it pleases us or brings to mind a significant association, or because its fascinating nature has touched us and brings us new inspiration.

Diamond

The diamond, the king of precious stones, also belongs to the Crown Center. It consists of pure carbon and is the hardest known mineral. It must be ground extensively in order for its perfect radiant power to be fully manifested. And therefore it also initiates processes in us that grind and shape our essence.

As the hardest of stones it also lends us the power of invincibility. It stood the tests of grinding and polishing without being broken by them. On the contrary, because it did, its shining, sparkling radiance becomes visible.

But the diamond will also make us aware of »hardness« in ourselves that can rapidly become a dark armor surrounding us. The greatest danger in wearing diamonds is therefore that of becoming arrogant, rejecting and taciturn, of elevating oneself above others.

If, however, we are on the path of self-knowledge and therefore prepared to work on the negative aspects of our personality, and instead of fighting them in ourselves and others to approach them with faith in higher guidance and divine love, the hardness will increasingly dissolve, and whatever is obscuring the perfect radiance in us will be »ground away«.

With it a purification of the highest degree will set in, that gradually lets us cast off more and more of the egocentric patterns of thought and behavior that prove useless to us, so that the separation between »I« and »you« is overcome and undivided, universal consciousness becomes possible.

The diamond is the expression of highest purity, clarity and enlightenment. It sends out the clear, bright and divine light that unites all colors in itself, that was in creation at the beginning, before it divided itself into the color spectrum of denser vibrations. To this light we shall return when we have learned our lessons completely, and the control over matter and spirit has returned to our being to be used and unfolded further for the benefit of all of creation.

The Energy Centers

of the Hands and Feet

In the palms of our hands and the middle of the soles of our feet the so-called secondary energy centers are located, the points at which the body's energy channels end.

Our feet are what we stand on the ground with, and beneath their soles an exchange of energy with the Earth takes place. This is our connection with the Earth, a taking on and giving off of energy, the rooting in earthly processes and the inclusion of spiritual powers and realizations into existance on the material plane.

For this the realm of precious stones offers us two helpers: the snowflake obsidian and tourmaline quartz, both of which unite the polarity of the bright and the dark, shadow and light.

Snowflake Obsidian

The snowflake obsidian is a black, opaque stone speckled with white or grey spots reminiscent of snowflakes or clouds. It lends us a psychic power that we experience as a rooting in Mother Earth, and provides us with stability and steadfastness when we are shaken by the storms of life.

This obsidian can be of great help to anyone tending to flights into spiritual dimensions that lead to losing touch with reality and one's solid footing. With its black base color it symbolizes the »denseness« of matter and the power of the Earth, and with its white flecks the spiritual light. In this way it teaches us not to see the path to spiritual knowledge as something removed from everyday life, but rather to make daily living a realm of spiritual experience, so that our spiritual and material needs do not remain separate from one another — which, lastly, they cannot be — so that one finds expression in the other.

We might place a small snowflake obsidian or tourmaline quartz in our stockings or shoes so that we will be directly connected with these vibrations and in feeling the stone will be reminded to direct our attention towards our feet, which are the opposite pole to our head and therewith to our mental processes.

This also helps prevent cold feet, which are an indication of our not being properly grounded and are not maintaining the proper harmony between spirit and matter. Increased energy will flow wherever we direct our thoughts and feelings. Usually we scatter our energy by letting our thoughts wander uncontrolled instead of consciously focussing them on what we are doing at the moment. When we learn to be where we are completely, we can holistically grasp the full measure of beauty, vitality and joy inherent in creation, and live fulfilled.

Tourmaline Quartz

In tourmaline quartz two types of stone are united: it is rock crystal containing black thread-like inclusions of tourmaline. They have experienced a mutual growth process in not separating but instead joining with one another in such a way that the individuality of the one mineral accentuates that of the other. Both stones also occur separately in nature, but in this combined configuration they teach us not to reject or fight the opposite, but to enhance its expression harmoniously and in mutual respect for the other's beauty.

So tourmaline quartz, too, is a stone that unites polarities in itself, but in a way opposite to that of the snowflake obsidian. With its clear crystalline power of light it envelops the dark tourmaline needles – the spirit having come to the matter.

This is a stone for very earth-bound people that are so occupied with material wishes and goals that they hardly align themselves with the highest goals of the soul. But it is also a great help to those who want to open themselves to the »Light of the Soul«, whose wish it is to fill their lives far more with spiritual content, and suffer from the fact that they still cling too much to material desires and security.

With its crystalline, light-filled vibrations it also corresponds with those souls who came to this Earth with a great deal of light in order to spread it for the benefit and growth of all Creation.

With the tourmaline we learn to accept our weaknesses and faults, so that they can change for the good and turn to strengths. Thereby we learn life's fundamental wisdom and discover which forms they take here on Earth and how they express themselves. We no longer transfer our difficulties onto others because we can feel that it is our own patterns that we project and reject, when we become aware of them.

With this realization there finally are
– no people bearing us ill will,
– no plants seeking to harm us,
– no animals intending to beset us,
– no stones that are either positive or negative,
– no spirit beings to be made responsible for our own fears and addictions,

but instead only the knowledge, that the entire universe is vibration and resonance, and that likes attract each other. When we are sad, everything can nourish and intensify this vibration. If we are filled with joy, we constantly happen upon more joy. So by ceaseless thinking, feeling, wanting and acting we ourselves decide what kind of vibrations we produce and radiate, and what consequentially we will attract to ourselves.

The energy centers of the hands receive and emit energies that come from the soul, and the right hand gives while the left hand receives. Through them the universal power of life flows when we healingly lay on our hands with the awareness of being a channel for divine love.

These centers correspond with the rock crystal, a very special mineral which also provides all of the other energy centers with purification, clarity, energy and enlightenment.

Rock Crystal

Rock crystal is a stone that spreads harmony, the power of love, clarity, purity and light wherever it happens to be and thereby lights up the entire atmosphere. In resonance to the divine light it vibrates in every being and touches upon the divine light of our soul, letting it radiate clear and bright, and increases our yearning to be totally permeated by this light, this purity, clearness and divine wisdom. In the colorless bright light of the rock crystal the entire power of Creation is present, undivided and unbroken.

We can place the crystal on every area of our bodies or assign it to any energy center, which it will then bring a brightening of the color vibration and with it a refining, easing, loosening, purifying and charging of the functions of that particular center. (Refer especially to the Inner Eye Center). Or else we place it on a painful spot where it brings relief that may let the pain disappear altogether.

If we place rock crystal in our aura, the energy field that surrounds us and vibrates in all of the colors of the rainbow, the colors will also become brighter — a purification and charge. Burdensome vibrations that are present in the aura before they manifest themselves as illnesses in the body or psyche, are dissolved by the crystal's vibrations, penetrated by its light and guided away.

There are many possibilities of utilizing the crystal as a bringer of light as well as for the concentration and charging of energy. Here a few examples:

If we place the crystal in our living room or bedroom, perhaps at a window, on a desk, close to flowers, on the nightstand oder beneath the bed, it will bring the vibrations of harmony and peace to the room because it can interrupt and change disruptive energy fields, and harmonize and intensify our sleep.

When we place a crystal beneath our pillow it clears our thoughts while we sleep and accompanies and protects our dreams and the wanderings of our soul into other dimensiosn with its light.

We can bury crystals beneath trees or in a garden and in this manner give them back to the Earth. In this way we give the vegetable kingdom healing, stimulating energy from the cosmic world, and help sick trees and forests to recover. We should let ourselves be inspired and led by the crystals — they will show us where and how to utilize them.

Chapter III

Meditations and Treatments Using Gemstones and Crystals

Whether we receive a new stone or a piece of jewelry or begin or end a meditation with one of our minerals, we should conduct a ceremony of purification and recharging in every instance. But the stones that we wear or have around us should be treated with this ritual from time to time.

Peoples closely connected to nature do this by placing their stones in running water for several days and then laying them out in the sun. This procedure is rarely feasable for us in our environment, and therefore we should create and practise new rituals in keeping with our times and circumstances.

The stones themselves taught me to use my powers of imagination, which through my thought streams and visualizations let me achieve results that are at least as effective as an actual treatment — the spirit forms matter. Attitude and dedication are deciding, as in all other areas of life.

Cleansing and Charging

The cleansing ceremony:

We take one or more stones or a piece of jewelry in our hands, close our eyes and »see« the stones before our inner eye. Then we visualize taking them to a waterfall or to a pure, clear spring and immerse them in the water. In our inner sight everything burdensome, dirty and dark is removed from the stones and swept away by the water.

The charging ceremony:

As soon as we »see« the stones as being cleansed and pure, we open our hands and imagine ourselves holding the stones up to the sun that dries them, lets them shine in their full splendor and charges them with its light.

In the course of this visualization we may also hold our stones under cold flowing water and then dry them with a clean cloth made of natural fibers.

Wearing and Storing Gemstones

We should not keep precious stones in dark boxes or safes, but rather in special places where they will be in our field of vision frequently.

Stones with which we meditate, that we wear or simply want to have near us, we can arrange in form of a mandala on a pleasing piece of cloth, on a table, in a niche, on a window-sill, a nightstand, a desk or work table, in a bowl or a seashell.

In any case the stones should be kept in the open so that their energy fields can unfold fully. It is also important where they are placed and how we carry them on our person. Once we have accepted them as friends and helpers in our life, they begin to share themselves with us. We then sense very precisely, which stone helps us with what the best, which one we keep near us during the day by wearing or carrying it, which one we place under our pillow or want near us as we work.

When we grow closer to the stones we learn to consciously live with their and our own energy vibrations, and on this basis to pick the jewelry or single stones for our days, our nights, certain situations, a problem or an illness.

Stones whose vibrations have a healing or helpful effect on the first energy centers, are best kept in a pants pocket. All others will be most effective in the area of our neck or heart region. But there are exceptions. We can determine the area of effectiveness by the length of the chain or cord on which we wear a stone: stones worn on a longer chain will affect the Heart Center or the Navel Center, while those on shorter chains will influence the Throat Center and from there the Inner Eye Center and the Crown Center.

Gemstone Meditations

Phase of Attunement

In order to consciously turn our complete attention inward and connect with the stones' subtle powers, we should withdraw to a place free of distraction so that we can concentrate fully on what is about to happen: our opening ourselves and becoming one with the vibrations of the stones.

Positions for Meditation

1. We lie on our back in a relaxed and serene state of mind. The legs are parallel, never crossed, and the arms lie next to the body, and not accross the chest or abdomen. If we feel like it, we can cover ourselves with a cloth. And sometimes it can be helpful to let meditation music play.

2. Or else we meditate in a sitting position and place a stone on our Crown Center, or one stone in each of the energy center of the hands. We may also prefer to arrange a number of selected stones in a mandala on a cloth in front of us.

Meditation Instructions

At the outset we should establish an inner connection with the stones, take them in our hands and visualize their being cleansed and charged, as described previously. Then we ask the stones and divine love — or whatever we wish to call this powerful energy — for help and protection and place one or more stones on our body or in the aura, and let the energy of their vibrations act on us for ten to thirty mintes. They will ease tension wherever it may have built up and provide energy where it is lacking.

If during meditation a stone changes position due to subtlest impulses of our body, we can assume that our body has caused this (unconsciously). We should therefore make no (conscious) effort to put it back in its previous place, not even if it has rolled off and is now lying beside us. It will still be within our aura and continues to vibrate there. Through the body's inherent intelligence and our higher »guidance« we know best, where the stone can be most effective for us.

Suggestions for Meditation

We select stones that sparkle at us and correspond to the colors of the energy centers and place them on the proper center area of the body:

Energy Centers

7th Energy Center – violet
6th Energy Center – dark blue
5th Energy Center – light blue
4th Energy Center – pink + green
3rd Energy Center – yellow + yellow-brown
2nd Energy Center – orange
1st Energy Center – red + reddish brown

Energy Centers of the feet: Snowflake obsidian or tourmaline quartz
Energy Centers of the hands: Rock crystal

● We select rock crystals only and place one on each of the energy centers as well as in our hands (or beneath them) and by our feet (at the heels).
● We take a rock crystal or a rutilated quartz and place it on a part of the body that is painful or stressed.
● We select a stone for a particular energy center and place it there, for example

− a violet, white or clear fluorite-octahedron on the Crown Center
− a rock crystal or lapis lazuli on the Inner Eye Center
− a blue topaz on the Throat Center
− a rhodonite or malachite on the Heart Center
− a citrine on the Solar Plexus Center
− a carnelian on the Sacral Center
− a jasper on the Base Center
− a rock crystal or polished sphere thereof on the energy centers of the hands
− a snowflake obsidian between the heels, so that it radiates to the energy centers of the feet.

When we have completed the meditation we should assume a humble, thankful position: we let our heart speak and give thanks for the divine help and the power of the stones.

Finally, we again take the stones in our hands and enact the visualized cleansing and charging. In doing so we may hold them under running water and dry them with a cloth, so that afterwards we can return them to their places in their pure, charged state.

»Dance« of Activation

By walking around and through a gemstone-mandala laid out as shown below, we can activate our total energy considerably, return that which is burdensome to the Earth and gather new strength:

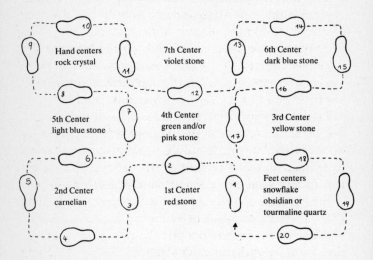

We move through the energy field of the stones repeatedly using twenty steps, and imagine while we are doing it a beam of light emitted by each stone shining straight up, which we do not touch with our body, so that we traverse the energy field in an erect and very conscious manner.

Our hands are angled away from the body, as if the palms were resting on a spiritual »water«, a sea of light.

By negotiating this Path of Power we gather a great

deal of energy that refreshes, revitalizes and encourages us. But through hesitation in our movement, unsteadiness, or uncertainty with the next step, it will also show us where we are out of balance at the moment. Through regular practise such problems or blockades will be treated and changed by the vibrations of the stones. We can feel what is happening when our pace changes, our steps become slower or faster, or when we tighten the pattern of the stones.

At the end we stand with slightly parted legs over the stones in the middle, which correspond to our heart center and rest, sense the flow of energy in us, the impressions and insights that arise in us.

Intuitively choosing a stone to step over we leave the energy field, and can receive a message from the center of the stone by which we left — for instance, that we receive additional strength for the solving of a matter that occupies us, a problem or an illness from this particular center, or that this center contains something that we should be working on.

When we place the stones on the ground or floor, we should do it with inner dedication. As we hold the stones in our hands we cleanse and charge them as described previously and ask for their help, for divine guidance and strength, and see ourselves infused and surrounded by light, enveloped in an oval of light edged with gold.

After completing the »dance« of activation we give thanks, cleanse the stones and charge them, and again see ourselves in the gilt-edged »egg« of light. We may, if we wish, let the stones remain in this constellation on the ground or floor for daily use.

Treatment With Gemstones

We can support the effectiveness of the gemstones by making ourselves into a channel for divine love and the universal flow of life, and standing by others with the healing, helping energy of the stones, thusly treating them. This can be approached in a number of ways. The few selected examples given here are merely meant to serve as stimuli.

The basis of every treatment should be the following procedure:

Selection of the stones / ritual of cleansing and charging / attunement, accompanied by the request to be permitted to be a channel for the universal life force, and asking for spiritual guidance, protection and assistance of the stones / treatment with gemstones / thanking / ritual of cleansing and charging

Balancing the Energy Centers by Their Colors and Those of the Gemstones

Generally speaking, there are two approaches to treatment:
− We talk with our partner and jointly determine which stone or stones will be employed in treatment.

- If one is familiar with the pendulum or other instruments that relate subtle energy vibrations, they can be implemented to determine suitable stones.

We then have our partner lie down comfortable in a place free of disturbances, cover him or her if it seems appropriate, and make sure the he or she assumes the proper position described previously.

We close our eyes and let go of everything that has occupied us up until then, and concentrate our attention in ourselves. The person performing the treatment cleanses the stones in his or her hands and charges them via visualization: a waterfall or spring and sunlight, as stated before. While doing this, the stones may be held under running water and then dried with a cloth.

The administering person asks the mineral kingdom to unfold its powers and requests that God provide guidance and protection for oneself and for the partner to be treated. One requests to be permitted to be a pure channel of divine love, divine light, the universal life force or however we wish to call this source of strength — but without calling forth additional images. This would predetermine the flow of infinite divine wisdom and limit it. One should maintain the attitude that the »universal life force« itself knows best what this human being lying before us in devotion and trust needs now, and that the energy will flow through us best when we give up our conscious imagining and simply put ourselves at the disposal of divine power. It can then flow unhindered through the administering person and affect in the person to be treated precisely what may happen in harmony with his or her being and divine will. The gemstones that are applied will work accordingly.

For the protection of both persons involved, the one administering should visualize them infused and surrounded by the gilt-edged egg of light. That will prevent undesired beings or forces gaining entry to our energy field and perhaps causing symptons of illness, pain or states of fatigue.

Now the administrating person places the stones on the partner to be treated and then places both hands with fingers extended and joined on the stone lying on the lowest energy center. There a vital flow of divine energy will be felt streaming through the hands. This flow is usually perceived as a feeling of warmth or a tingling sensation. In this manner the energy vibrations of the stones and the centers are transformed once more through the universal divine healing energy flowing through the hands.

When the warmth or tingling in the hands subsides, or an »inner voice« says ›Enough!‹, the hands are moved to the next higher energy center and held there, until the flow of energy ebbs away. This is continued until the 7th energy center has been treated.

In treating the centers of the throat, inner eye or crown, one may sense it to be better not to lay the hands on directly. In this case the hands do not touch the skin, but are held into the energy field of the aura instead. These last three energy centers are particularly sensitive and are pervaded by more subtle vibrations.

The person administering should always insure that the fingers are joined and the hands rest next to each other, so that energies are not scattered, but instead will be transferred and centered optimally.

After treating the 7th energy center the administering person sits upright and gives thanks to the mineral kingdom for its assistance, and to the universal life force for being permitted to be its channel. Then he or she again visualizes both persons in the egg of light with the golden edge, and touches the treated person on the feet or shoulders in order to recall it from its altered state of consciousness – also known as an alpha state, state of relaxation or trance – and to ground it.

Only then does the administering person take the stones off the other, holds them in the hands in order to visualize their cleasing, and perhaps holds them under cold running water in order to then dry them with a cloth and lovingly return them to their places.

After a gemstone-treatment has been administered, discussion between the partners is often helpful and may, indeed, be necessary in order to process the experiences made, which can be of high intensity, and to help integrate them into conscious everyday life.

A gemstone-treatment should never be ended prior to this stage, and one should also never leave the partner lying alone and unattended with stones on the body.

This type of gemstone-treatment not only leads to a charging of the energy centers with new vibration power, it also brings them into harmony. This can put the treated person in touch with partial aspects of his or her personality that have been blocking harmony, but are ready to open themselves up and communicate. Not only does this permit beneficial, joyous feelings to arise, we are also confronted by our own »shadow sides«, but essential about this is, that they are offering to be solved and to become »sunny sides« once the process of acceptance has been completed. The universal life force and the powers of the stones help us achieve this.

In a way, nothing is changed. Afterwards we have no more nor less of a given weakness, our way of viewing things, energy, or an aspect of our personality, but instead everything will be adjusted within the framework of what we have by nature, it will be brought into balance or into motion: energy is activated (in the case of lethargy), or energy may be sublimated (as in the case of pain).

Remote Healing Meditation
Using Rock Crystal

We retreat to a quiet place free of disturbances and take a rock crystal into our hands, clease and charge it, get attuned to it, and ask to be permitted to be a channel for the universal life force, the divine light and the love for a person whom we wish to help. We name the person we are thinking of and ask the crystal in our hands to send him or her the universal life force. Then we visualize ourselves enveloped in an egg of light edged in gold, and then proceed to the other person with a shining beam of the crystal. The recipient is infusing his or her body more and more with light, and then the aura begins to glow, and its outer perimeter of shining vibrations end in gold. As soon as we have completely surrounded the other person with our gilt-edged egg of light, we we retain this visualization for awhile with our inner eye and in our imagination are connected with this person.

In this case, too, as in direct treatment, we should not conceive a desired healing, but instead leave this up to the universal life force. Our own concepts, and be they ever so helpfully and well intended, infringe on the flow of the universal life force. We can be certain that this force will reach the other person, will become effective and will work changes.

When we wish to end the meditation, we should disconnect the shining beam from the other person and let it return to the crystal. We then again see ourselves within the gilt-edged egg of light, give thanks to the

crystal and the life energy for their help, cleanse the crystal and charge it, and return it to its place.

Through remote healing with crystals we can utilize the world of subtle vibrations to support people who have asked for our help or whom we love.

But by these means we can also enter into connections with plants, trees, forests, lakes, rivers, animals and more.

The Healing Circle Using Crystals

When an entire group of people gets together for the purpose of meditation, the energies involved can multiply and concentrate enormously.

We stand or sit in a circle, with each person holding a rock crystal in his or her hands. The person wishing to be energized sits in the center of the circle.

The ceremony or ritual begins:

We attune ourselves, cleanse the crystal and charge it, ask to be permitted to be a channel for the universal life force, envelop ourselves in a gilt-edged egg of light, and then take up contact with the rock crystal and visualize a light that is emitted by it and streams to the person in the center, so that he or she is totally pervaded and surrounded by this light. We »see« him or her in an egg of light edged in gold and we retain this image.

If the meditation is to be ended, we intensely concentrate on this image once more and then let the beam of light return to the rock crystal. While doing this, we see ourselves in the egg of light, thank the crystal and the life force for their help, cleanse the crystal and

The Healing Circle

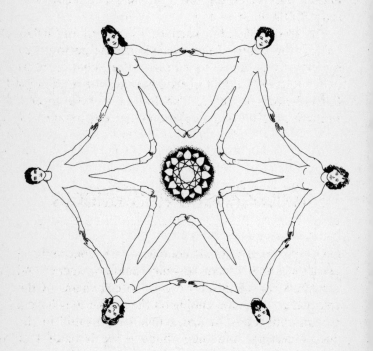

charge it, and perhaps repeat the Healing Circle with another person in the center.

Using the Healing Circle we may, however, send the crystal light to people, animals, plants, etc. that are not present. In order to do this, all members of the circle agree on an identical image. Everyone visualizes it in the center of the circle and lets the light flow through himself and the crystal, until the image is totally infused with the light.

The »spiritual world« carries these vibrations further on into the realm of the universe, to the person they are meant for, or else to the place where there is resonance, such as all the forests if we have the image of a forest before our eyes. The forests thereby receive strength to fulfill their purpose and to regenerate.

Experiences and Effects

Gemstones and Crystals contain subtle, concentrated energies that let them become channels, agents and catalyzers, or whatever we wish to call them, of the spiritual powers. Depending on their color they have a certain connection to and a function to fulfill in the energy centers, and their shape – be it natural or ground and polished – and size provide a differentiated basic alignment and purpose. Thereby they draw vibrations of the same resonance from the entire cosmos unto themselves – and place them at our disposal.

Here I would like to recall for you a small sampling of selected case studies regarding the effects of gemstones in my own practise:

● A carnelian helped a woman who had long been suffering from a sickness of the lymphatic system. Even lymph drainage had failed to ease her condition. Within a week after she began constantly carrying the carnelian on her person, she began urinating extensively and her legs began to grow slimmer. The carnelian disappeared after this week and was not found again. A citrine then continued to help her stabilize her metabolism. Since then she has been sleeping well and her digestion is as regular as never before. Besides this, the citrine helped her to sell her store, which she had been trying to do for a long time, within two weeks following brief negotiations. A day after the contract was signed, the citrine disappeared. She now wears a malachite to help her clear her personal situation. Difficulties she had had with her heart have since disappeared.

● A chrysocolla »sacrificed« itself for a man who had to begin life all over again following major brain surgery. He had to relearn speaking, walking, writing and controlling his body and its functions. A rehabilitation center from which he had expected extensive support informed him that he could count on space in three months time at the earliest. The chrysocolla that came to his help so that he would not immerse himself in self-pity but instead would find his way back into an active life, for no apparent reason burst into pieces in the hand of his wife when she brought it to him from me. A few days later he was notified by the rehabilitation center that he could come immediately, as a place had surprisingly become available.

- A rock crystal that had been placed on a desk in order to improve the relationship with the superior broke when this same person picked it up to look at it and dropped it. This made a profound impression on the superior. A new level of communication marked the relationship of the two men, who up until then had been very aggressive and competitive with each other. A new rock crystal brought them mutual consideration and respect.

- A red jasper the size of a palm of a hand caused extreme labor pains in a woman who had put it on her belly during meditation. She was thrown back to the birth of her last child, which had been overshadowed by fear and which she had not yet processed in herself. Following this experience she was able to have a much more relaxed relationship with her child. Abdominal pains and irregularities in her menstrual cycle disappeared after a while.

- A malachite caused coronary pain and remembrances of his mother in a young man. Afterwards he was able to approach her in a new way.

- A chalcedony enabled a man to give a speech in front of an audience of a hundred listeners, which he had up until then considered impossible for himself.

- Chalcedony and the blue-dyed agate have provided a number of people with the will-power to stop smoking.

In meditation, gemstones and crystals give us experiences with their pure, strong vibrations, in the course of which we see a great deal of light and glowing colors, and are given the opportunity of experiencing oneness with them.

Their vibrations unite themselves with our being — they become a part of us. Even heavy stones that lie on our bodies soon dissolve into thin air, so to speak. We no longer feel their weight because we have totally united with them, and are carried by cosmic powers.

This experience of oneness is a goal of many religions and teachings of wisdom. The minerals give us this condition as a »present«, if our brain does not agitate against it or we shut ourselves off through our own projections and expectations.

Do not expect anything, let go and it will happen, and in the manner that is right for each of us in this very moment.

This may reveal itself in the crossing of new realms, other dimensions and experiences of light, but old pains may also rise to the surface. Injuries of body or soul can address us through images, feelings and thoughts; memories may suddenly re-awaken — to be viewed through other, more experienced eyes.

All of us today are no longer the helpless children we once were, children that felt suppressed, misunderstood, deprived, etc., that yearned for more love and understanding. And yet we often still react that way, as hurt and self-centered as we were then. The same way we sometimes defended ourselves then against our parents, siblings, friends and teachers ..., we are defending ourselves today against our partners, our own children, superiors, colleagues at work, etc. Only by honestly coming to terms with ourselves can we learn step by step to see and accept ourselves with all of our real desires, weaknesses and strengths, to demonstrate understanding, forgiveness and love towards ourselves and to develop these qualities for the benefit of those, whom we feel have somehow hurt us.

In this process the stones are the friends and allies that accompany us with the strong cosmic energies that they have concentrated in themselves.

Selflessly they assist us in the process of solving our everyday problems, the challenges life presents us, physical sickness, emotional hurt and mental rigidity – provide us the strength for new orientation, new attitudes and new relationships. These effects touch upon every aspect of our lives and call forth changes that we previously did not consider possible. This does not mean that the stones will remove all of the hurdles from our path and will simply make all difficulties disappear. But they do provide us with the strength we need to solve our problems, to dissolve old energy patterns from the realm of our thinking and feeling that have led to disharmony and illness.

And so space is created for new potential and goals. For this, too, the minerals provide us with the highest cosmic powers, which leads to the unfolding and strengthening of new, beneficial capabilities and to an expansion of consciousness – for the benefit of all of creation. Because what we do for ourselves, the way we live, how and what we think and feel, is projected far beyond our aura into the universe and connects with vibrations of the same kind. In this manner we gain contact with people whom we may have never met, but who, for example, experience the same cause of an illness. We can help them then through the vibrations that have been altered in us. On the other hand we attract energy patterns of this type given off by others. In this the direct principle of resonance is demonstrated, which is effective in the entire universe.

If we think, feel and act fearfully, we will be connected with all of the fearful vibrations on this Earth, which will concentrate our fears and make them stronger. If we successfully manage to make our fear into an attitude of confidence and trust, we will be connected with the corresponding vibrations of confidence and trust from the entire Earth.

If we turn to our higher providence and send out light and love, we will be connected to the entire spiritual world, which reacts to our message directly with all of the means at its disposal and is ready to help and to serve us, if we ask for that and devotedly apply ourselves from the very bottom of our heart.

We are therefore creators and masters of our lives, and we carry full responsibility for our being here as well as for the condition and development of the Earth and all of its beings, as all are part of the whole. The stones, too, are part of this entirety and fulfill their function as concrete helpers of the one true spirit here on Earth. What they can do for us depends on each of us individually.

»No one can give more than that,
which he has found in himself.«
(Hans Kruppa)

Angelika Höfler
I CHING
NEW SYSTEMS, METHODS
AND REVELATIONS
An innovative guide for all
of life's events and changes
190 Pages
ISBN 0-941524-37-X

Angelika Hoefler

I CHING

NEW SYSTEMS, METHODS
AND REVELATIONS
An innovative guide
for all of life's
events and changes

LOTUS LIGHT
SHANGRI-LA

The I Ching – with new methods, new possibilities and new answers.

The author, herself actively interested in esoterics, studied characterology and applied as well as experimental psychology autodidactically, and has brought the eastern wisdom of the I Ching into poignant, contemporary language that includes glimpses of a knowing smile. In order to achieve exact answers, the hexagrams were divided into themes of inquiry, so that we can also receive concrete information about our own psychological make-up and condition, that of others and aspects of partnership. Each hexagram is accompanied by specific advice that is especially valuable in that it augments the partial as well as complete hexagram information, but can be applied independently of it. But the highlight of Angelika Hoefler's work is her development of a symbiosis of the I Ching and the Cabbala of Numbers, with which she has created a completely new system of cognition, of recognition and therewith practical help in life. We receive information, teachings, warnings, encouragement or advice, e. g. in questions of the right profession, place of education, living, work or vacation. Or in questions about the influence that certain persons or dates, agreements, names or titles to be decided on by us may have our success in life. Additionally, we gain clarity about where we stand in life–and this perhaps for the first time ever–what our functions and tasks are, where we belong and who belongs to us, and what the other person thinks about us.

Monika Jünemann
ENCHANTING SCENTS
The Secrets of Aroma Therapy.
Fragrant Essences that stimulate,
activate and inspire body, mind
and spirit
128 Pages
ISBN 0-941524-36-1

This book will carry you away to the world of exquisite, enchanting scents. Various fragrances effect our moods, may stimulate and excite us or bring us calmness and harmony, can bewitch and inspire, or even heal. Since ancient times essential oils and incenses have been employed in healing, for seduction and for religious rituals.

Today we are as captivated by the magic of lovely scents and as irresistably captivated by them as ever. The effects that essential oils have can vary greatly. This book particularly treats their subtle influences, but also presents and describes the plants from which they are obtained. *Enchanting Scents* beckons you to enter the realm of sensual experience, to journey into the world of fragrance through essences.

It is an invitation to employ personal, individual scents, to activate body and spirit, and to let your imagination soar. Here is a key that will open your senses to the limitless possibilities of benefitting from fragrances as stimulators, sources of energy and means of healing, or simply to let them broaden the scope of your own perception.